THE BEST MLB
PITCHERS
OF ALL TIME

By Will Graves

Published by ABDO Publishing Company, PO Box 398166, Minneapolis, MN 55439. Copyright © 2014 by Abdo Consulting Group, Inc. International copyrights reserved in all countries. No part of this book may be reproduced in any form without written permission from the publisher. SportsZone™ is a trademark and logo of ABDO Publishing Company.

Printed in the United States of America,
North Mankato, Minnesota
102013
012014

Editor: Chrös McDougall
Series Designer: Christa Schneider

Photo credits: AP Images, cover (left), 1 (left), 7, 11, 15, 17, 19, 21, 25, 27, 31, 33, 41; Tammy Lechner/AP Images, cover (right), 1 (right); Bain Collection/Library of Congress, 9, 13; Charles Knoblock/AP Images, 23; John Rooney/AP Images, 29; Richard Drew/AP Images, 35, 37; Bill Ingraham/AP Images, 39; Gaylion Wampler/AP Images, 43; Susan Ragan/AP Images, 45; Peter Morgan/AP Images, 47; Jeff Zelevansky/AP Images, 49; John Bazemore/AP Images, 51; Brian Kersey/AP Images, 53; Paul Connors/AP Images, 55; Tom Hood/AP Images, 57; Chris O'Meara/AP Images, 59; Kathy Willens/AP Images, 61

Library of Congress Control Number: 2013945927

Cataloging-in-Publication Data
Graves, Will.
 The best MLB pitchers of all time / Will Graves.
   p. cm. -- (Major League Baseball's best ever)
Includes bibliographical references and index.
ISBN 978-1-62403-117-5
1. Major League Baseball (Organization)--Juvenile literature. 2. Pitching (Baseball)--Juvenile literature. 3. Pitchers (Baseball)--Juvenile literature.   I. Title.
796.357--dc23

                                        2013945927

TABLE OF CONTENTS

Introduction 4

Cy Young 6

Christy Mathewson 10

Walter Johnson 14

Bob Feller 18

Warren Spahn 22

Whitey Ford 26

Bob Gibson 30

Tom Seaver 34

Steve Carlton 38

Nolan Ryan 42

Roger Clemens 46

Greg Maddux 50

Randy Johnson 54

Mariano Rivera 58

Honorable Mentions 62

Glossary 63

For More Information 63

Index 64

About the Author 64

INTRODUCTION

Every play in baseball starts with the pitcher.

In Major League Baseball (MLB), pitchers control the pace of the game. They control the tone of the game. And in some instances, they control the entire game—either with a no-hitter or a perfect game. Great pitchers come in all sizes and have various specialties. Some pitchers thrive as flamethrowers who whip fastballs past helpless batters. Other pitchers rely on breaking balls, such as sliders, curveballs, and even knuckleballs. All that matters, though, is that they get the out.

Here are some of the best pitchers in MLB history.

CY YOUNG

Denton Young thought he had something to prove. It was 1890. He was playing for a team in Canton, Ohio. And he was throwing fastballs as hard as he could.

"I thought I had to show all my stuff, and I almost tore the boards off the grandstand with my fastball," Young said.

He earned the nickname "Cyclone" because of how hard he threw. The nickname was shortened to "Cy" when he moved to the major leagues later that year. It is a name that now stands for baseball greatness.

Young had a dominant fastball. Yet his work ethic might have been his best asset. Pitchers threw a lot more often in those days than they do now. And nobody worked harder than Young.

The Cy Young Awards are given annually to the best pitchers in each league.

He won 511 games during his 22-year career. That is a record that might never be broken. Young tossed one perfect game. That means no batter ever reached base. He also threw two other no-hitters.

Young was known for his fastball. But he didn't go for strikeouts. He hoped the ball would go to a fielder for an out. Young said that is what helped his arm stay fresh for so long.

Most pitchers in Young's era were done by age 30. But Young pitched until he was 44. His only World Series victory came in the first Fall Classic, in 1903. Young was elected to the Hall of Fame in 1937. And in 1956, the MLB created the Cy Young Award. Today it is given to the top pitcher every season in both the American League (AL) and the National League (NL).

15

The total number of times Young won more than 20 games in a season—the most ever by a pitcher.

Cy Young tosses warm-up pitches while with the Boston Red Sox in 1908.

CY YOUNG

Hometown: Gilmore, Ohio

Height, Weight: 6 feet 2, 210 pounds

Birth Date: March 29, 1867

Teams: Cleveland Spiders (1890–98)
St. Louis Perfectos/Cardinals (1899–1900)
Boston Americans/Red Sox (1901–08)
Cleveland Naps (1909–11)
Boston Rustlers (1911)

CHRISTY MATHEWSON

During a time when fierce competitors such as Ty Cobb played the game with a snarl, Christy Mathewson was different. Few baseball players went to college in the early 1900s. But Mathewson did. He attended Bucknell University. While there, he sang in the choir and even joined the football team.

On the baseball diamond, Mathewson mowed down batters with his fastball. Off the diamond, he wrote children's books. The ace pitcher became a role model both on and off the field.

Mathewson was a nice guy. But that did not mean he liked to lose. Maybe that is because he very rarely did. Mathewson was one of the greatest pitchers in baseball history. He won 373 games against just 188 losses.

Christy Mathewson dominated baseball during the 1900s and 1910s while playing mostly with the New York Giants.

Mathewson spent 17 seasons in the majors. Almost all of that time was with the New York Giants. In his career, Mathewson led the NL in victories four times. Today's top pitchers are lucky to win 20 games in a season. In 1908, Mathewson won 37.

Mathewson was even better in the World Series. His career earned-run average (ERA) in four World Series was 0.97. In the 1905 World Series, he tossed three shutouts. And the Giants won the title.

The secret to Mathewson's success was the way he studied the game. He remembered every pitch he threw. Then he made adjustments when a batter would find a way to get on base.

"Anytime someone got a hit off me, I always made a mental note of the pitch," Mathewson said. "He'd never see that one again."

79

The number of career shutouts by Mathewson— the third-most in baseball history through 2013, behind Walter Johnson and Pete Alexander.

Christy Mathewson warms up before pitching for the New York Giants in the 1911 World Series.

CHRISTY MATHEWSON

Hometown: Factoryville, Pennsylvania

Height, Weight: 6 feet 1, 195 pounds

Birth Date: August 12, 1880

Teams: New York Giants (1900–16)
Cincinnati Reds (1916)

WALTER JOHNSON

It was 1907. Walter Johnson was a rookie making his big league debut. And his lowly Washington Senators were up against the mighty Detroit Tigers. Washington lost the game. But Johnson managed to strike out Ty Cobb—one of the most feared hitters in the game.

"I hardly saw the pitch, but I heard it," Cobb said. "Every one of us knew we'd met the most powerful arm turned loose in a ballpark."

Cobb was right. During his 21-year career with Washington, Johnson dominated the AL. He earned the nickname "Big Train" because of his size and his mighty fastball. It was clocked at more than 91 miles per hour (146 km/h).

Washington Senators ace Walter Johnson warms up before a 1924 game.

The Senators were terrible for long stretches of Johnson's career. The only time they shined was when their ace pitcher was on the mound. Johnson won 417 games between 1907 and 1927. He also won the pitching "Triple Crown" three times. That means he led the AL in wins, ERA, and strikeouts in the same season.

0

The number of home runs Johnson allowed in 1916 despite pitching a whopping 369 2/3 innings. That is the record for most innings pitched in a season without giving up a homer.

Finally, near the end of Johnson's playing days, the Senators turned into a good team. They made it to the World Series in 1924. Johnson lost his first two appearances. His mother, Minnie, watched him pitch for the first time in Game 1 of the Fall Classic. Then he recovered to pitch the final four innings of Game 7. And Washington beat the New York Giants 4–3 to win the title.

Johnson retired in 1927. Through 2013, he still held the record for most career shutouts with 110.

Walter Johnson was one of the most feared pitchers in baseball for 21 seasons.

WALTER JOHNSON

Hometown: Humboldt, Kansas

Height, Weight: 6 feet 1, 200 pounds

Birth Date: November 6, 1887

Team: Washington Senators (1907–27)

Most Valuable Player (MVP) Awards: 1913, 1924

BOB FELLER

Baseball was not a complicated game to pitcher Bob Feller.

"I just reared back and let them go," he once said.

And nobody let them go faster than the player they called "Rapid Robert." The flame-throwing right-hander swamped batters with his remarkable fastball. There were no radar guns while Feller played for the Cleveland Indians from 1936 to 1956. That forced him to get creative in showcasing his speedy fastball.

One time Feller's fastball "raced" a police officer on a motorcycle. The officer raced by Feller going 86 miles per hour (138 km/h). Feller, who was wearing a shirt and tie, gave the officer a head start. The ball still beat the motorcycle to a target 60 feet, 6 inches (18.4 m) away from where Feller was standing.

Cleveland Indians pitcher Bob Feller throws a pitch during spring training in 1941.

Feller's powerful pitch helped him lead the AL in strikeouts seven times and win 266 games during his career. He probably could have won 300. But the United States entered World War II in 1941. Feller decided to serve his country in the US Navy.

He became a gunner on the USS *Alabama*. Feller even earned eight battle stars for his performance in combat.

The 26-year-old returned to the majors in 1945. And his fastball was as fast as ever. He helped the Indians reach the World Series in 1948. Then he led the AL in wins with 22 in 1951.

Feller tossed three no-hitters in his career. One of them came on Opening Day in 1940 against the Chicago White Sox. Through 2013 it remained the only time a major league pitcher no-hit an opponent on Opening Day.

4

The number of times Feller led the majors in walks. He said his wildness helped make him effective because batters were never sure where the ball was headed.

Indians pitcher Bob Feller delivers a pitch to home plate
during the 1948 World Series.

BOB FELLER

Hometown: Van Meter, Iowa

Height, Weight: 6 feet, 185 pounds

Birth Date: November 3, 1918

Team: Cleveland Indians (1936–41, 1945–56)*

All-Star Games: 1938, 1939, 1940, 1941, 1946,
1947, 1948, 1950

* Did not play 1942–44 because of military
service

WARREN SPAHN

Warren Spahn looked like he was dancing every time he pitched. The left-hander would kick his right leg high in the air before letting go of the ball. He did it to keep base runners from trying to steal and to hide the ball from batters before he threw the pitch.

It certainly worked.

Spahn used his funky delivery to become one of the greatest left-handers in baseball history. He won 363 games between 1942 and 1965—the most ever by a left-handed pitcher. Almost all of those wins came for the Boston and Milwaukee Braves. And they came thanks to his high-flying right leg and his brainy approach to the game he loved.

Spahn did not rely on a wicked fastball to be successful. Rather, he relied on his smarts.

The Milwaukee Braves' Warren Spahn hurls a pitch against the Los Angeles Dodgers in 1963.

**"A pitcher needs two pitches,"
Spahn said.** "One they're looking for and one to cross them up."

That worked for Spahn. He led the NL in strikeouts four straight times from 1949 to 1952. Yet he became even more successful later in his career. As a veteran, he focused more on getting batters to make weak contact rather than trying to strike them out. He won at least 21 games in every season between 1957 and 1961. And he captured the Cy Young Award in 1957.

Spahn was also one of the most durable pitchers of his generation. He tossed 382 complete games in his career. St. Louis Cardinals star Stan Musial once joked that Spahn would never get into the Hall of Fame because "he'll never stop pitching."

Spahn eventually did retire in 1965 as a 14-time All-Star and did become a Hall of Famer.

5,243 2/3

The number of innings Spahn pitched in his career—the most by an NL player through 2013.

Warren Spahn, *center*, celebrates with Boston Braves teammates after winning Game 5 of the 1948 World Series.

WARREN SPAHN

Hometown: Buffalo, New York

Height, Weight: 6 feet, 172 pounds

Birth Date: April 23, 1921

Teams: Boston Braves (1942, 1946–52)*
   Milwaukee Braves (1953–64)
   New York Mets (1965)
   San Francisco Giants (1965)

All-Star Games: 1947, 1949, 1950, 1951, 1952, 1953, 1954, 1956, 1957, 1958, 1959, 1961, 1962, 1963

Cy Young Award: 1957
*Did not play 1943–45 because of military service

WHITEY FORD

Nothing bothered Edward Charles Ford on the pitcher's mound. Not the opponent. Not the score. Not the stakes. The guy nicknamed "Whitey" because of his light blonde hair never seemed rattled. The bigger the game, the calmer he felt.

"He pitched his game," New York Yankees teammate Mickey Mantle said. "Cool. Crafty. Nerves of steel."

Maybe it was because Ford had so much practice. There have been better pitchers in baseball history. But none thrived quite the way Ford did when everything was on the line. The Yankees great was the ace for one of baseball's best dynasties. He helped the Yankees reach the World Series 11 times between 1950 and 1964. And New York won the championship six times during Ford's career.

New York Yankees ace Whitey Ford hurls a pitch to a Baltimore Orioles batter in 1961.

Ford won 236 regular-season games during his career. He said he could have won more if he had taken better care of himself. Still, the left-hander always managed to be at his best in October. He still held nearly every major World Series pitching record through 2013.

The records ranged from starts (22), to wins (10), to strikeouts (94). During one stretch, he threw a record 33 2/3 straight scoreless innings during the Fall Classic.

How important was Ford to the Yankees? They might have lost the 1960 World Series because he did not pitch enough. Rather than start in Game 1, he was held out until Game 3 against the underdog Pittsburgh Pirates. Ford tossed shutouts in both Game 3 and Game 6. But he was not available in Game 7 as the Pirates rallied to pull the upset.

.690

Ford's career winning percentage (236–106)—the highest in baseball history by a pitcher with more than 300 career decisions.

Whitey Ford pitches for the Yankees in Game 4 of the 1950 World Series against the Philadelphia Phillies.

WHITEY FORD

Hometown: New York, New York

Height, Weight: 5 feet 10, 178 pounds

Birth Date: October 21, 1928

Team: New York Yankees (1950, 1953–67)*

All-Star Games: 1954, 1955, 1956, 1958, 1959, 1960, 1961, 1964

Cy Young Award: 1961

*Did not play 1951–52 because of military service

BOB GIBSON

Long before Bob Gibson became the toughest pitcher in baseball, he was a sick child growing up in Nebraska. One time, he felt so ill he was sent to the hospital. His older brother, Josh, came to visit him. Josh promised his little brother that if he started feeling better, Josh would buy him a baseball glove.

It was an offer that changed Gibson's life. He soon recovered from his illness. And sure enough, Josh bought him a glove and taught his little brother how to play. The rest is history.

Gibson grew into one of the most consistent pitchers of his generation. He won 251 games and two Cy Young Awards during his career with the St. Louis Cardinals. And he was at his best in the World Series. The Cardinals won the series twice during Gibson's career. In 1967, Gibson basically won it by himself.

St. Louis Cardinals pitcher Bob Gibson throws a three-hitter to beat the Boston Red Sox in Game 7 of the 1967 World Series.

Gibson started Games 1, 4, and 7 against the Boston Red Sox during that World Series. The Cardinals won all three games, including a 7–2 victory in Game 7 to win it all.

Gibson won by throwing hard and protecting his turf. That was especially true if a batter had just gotten a home run. Gibson would send a message the next time the batter was at the plate. He would pitch the ball hard and inside, sending the batter stumbling out of the way.

"I want to be remembered as a person, a competitor, that gave 100 percent every time I went out on the field," Gibson said.

1.12

Gibson's ERA during the 1968 season—the lowest ERA for a full season since 1914.

The Cardinals' Bob Gibson fires a pitch during Game 1 of the 1968 World Series against the Detroit Tigers.

BOB GIBSON

Hometown: Omaha, Nebraska

Height, Weight: 6 feet 1, 189 pounds

Birth Date: November 9, 1935

Team: St. Louis Cardinals (1959–75)

All-Star Games: 1962, 1965, 1966, 1967, 1968, 1969, 1970, 1972

Cy Young Awards: 1968, 1970

Gold Gloves: 1965, 1966, 1967, 1968, 1969, 1970, 1971, 1972, 1973

MVP Award: 1968

TOM SEAVER

Growing up in California, Tom Seaver loved to play baseball with his dad, Charles. Charles did not like to pitch though. He left that up to his son. And the younger Seaver developed into a three-time Cy Young Award winner and one of the best big-game pitchers of all time.

Seaver began his career playing for the lowly New York Mets. The Mets had always been losers when Seaver joined the team in 1967. Two years later, though, they were World Series champions. Seaver helped make sure of that.

"There are two places in baseball," Seaver said. "First place and no place."

And there was no place like first place for Seaver. He won 25 games in 1969 as the "Amazin' Mets" rallied late in the season to win the NL East and then the pennant.

New York Mets pitcher Tom Seaver sends a pitch to the plate during the 1983 season opener.

They then went on to defeat the heavily favored Baltimore Orioles in the World Series. Seaver held the mighty Orioles to just six hits while pitching 10 innings in a 2–1 victory in Game 4. The Mets won it all the next day.

That season made Seaver a superstar. The player nicknamed "Tom Terrific" became one of the steadiest pitchers of his time. He won at least 16 games 12 different times. And he picked up his 300th victory while pitching for the Chicago White Sox in 1985.

Seaver retired after the 1986 season. When his name was on the ballot for the Hall of Fame in 1992, he collected a higher percentage of votes than any player in baseball history.

"If you dwell on statistics, you get shortsighted," Seaver said. "If you aim for consistency, the numbers will be there at the end."

16

The number of Opening Day starts Seaver made during his career—the most in baseball history through 2013.

Tom Seaver won three Cy Young Awards during his 12 seasons with the New York Mets.

TOM SEAVER

Hometown: Fresno, California

Height, Weight: 6 feet 1, 195 pounds

Birth Date: November 17, 1944

Teams: New York Mets (1967–77, 1983)
Cincinnati Reds (1977–82)
Chicago White Sox (1984–86)
Boston Red Sox (1986)

All-Star Games: 1967, 1968, 1969, 1970, 1971,
1972, 1973, 1975, 1976, 1977, 1978, 1981

Cy Young Awards: 1969, 1973, 1975

Rookie of the Year: 1967

STEVE CARLTON

Steve Carlton was mad. He had just won 20 games for the St. Louis Cardinals in 1971. But the team still decided to trade him to the lowly Philadelphia Phillies. The Phillies were one of the worst teams in baseball when Carlton arrived. He was determined to help them turn around, though.

It took awhile. The Phillies won just 59 games during Carlton's first season. And 27 of those wins came when Carlton was on the pitcher's mound. The big, quiet guy they called "Lefty" won the first of his four Cy Young Awards that year. It was one of the most stunning seasons by a pitcher for such a bad team.

"I consider that season my finest individual achievement," Carlton said.

Team success soon followed. Carlton became the rock around which the Phillies built. By the late 1970s, Philadelphia was in the playoffs regularly.

Steve Carlton of the Philadelphia Phillies winds up to throw a pitch against the Cincinnati Reds in 1972.

In 1980, the Phillies finally won it all. Carlton started Game 6 of the World Series against the Kansas City Royals. He allowed just one run during seven-plus innings as Philadelphia celebrated a championship.

Though the Phillies were winners, Carlton never looked like he enjoyed playing. The slider specialist was known to be so focused when he pitched that he did not listen to his teammates or his coaches. Carlton said his concentration is what set him apart. He was so determined to put away each batter he would block out everything else.

That determination helped Carlton win 329 games during his career. That was still the second-highest total by a left-handed pitcher in baseball history through 2013. Not bad for a player who spent parts of his career on one of the worst teams in the majors.

4,136

The number of strikeouts Carlton recorded in his career—the fourth-highest total through 2013.

The Phillies' Steve Carlton pitches against the Los Angeles Dodgers during the 1978 playoffs.

STEVE CARLTON

Hometown: Miami, Florida

Birth Date: December 22, 1944

Height, Weight: 6 feet 4, 210 pounds

Teams: St. Louis Cardinals (1965–71)
Philadelphia Phillies (1972–86)
San Francisco Giants (1986)
Chicago White Sox (1986)
Cleveland Indians (1987)
Minnesota Twins (1987–88)

All-Star Games: 1968, 1969, 1971, 1972, 1974, 1977, 1979, 1980, 1981, 1982

Cy Young Awards: 1972, 1977, 1980, 1982

NOLAN
RYAN

There are fastballs, and then there are Nolan Ryan fastballs. Ryan's heater would dip and dart around the plate. Sometimes it was a ball. Sometimes it was a strike. Every time, though, it was blazing—a pitch so good it earned its own nickname, "The Ryan Express."

And just like a freight train, it was pretty hard to stop.

Ryan did not do anything fancy. He just reared back his powerful right arm and threw the ball as hard as he could. And more often than not, that was enough.

Hitters had two choices: watch the ball cross the plate and hope to draw a walk, or take a swing and hope to get lucky. They usually did not.

Nolan Ryan's fastball was so fast it earned the nickname "The Ryan Express."

Ryan struck out 5,714 batters in his career. That is a record that might never be broken. Only one player, Randy Johnson, had even come within 1,000 strikeouts of that mark through 2013. When facing Ryan, the batters always knew what was coming. They just could not do much about it.

Just as staggering as Ryan's fastball was his durability. He played for nearly three decades for four teams. Yet he appeared to get better as he got older. He tossed a record seven no-hitters, including one each in 1990 and 1991, when he was 43 and 44 years old.

Despite all those fastballs, Ryan never won the Cy Young Award. He did not need to win it, though, to be recognized as one of the all-time greats. Ryan was elected to the baseball Hall of Fame in 1999 with the second-highest percentage of votes in history.

7

The number of no-hitters Ryan pitched in his career. The next best pitcher had four.

Houston Astros ace Nolan Ryan pitches against the New York Mets during the 1986 playoffs.

NOLAN RYAN

Hometown: Refugio, Texas

Height, Weight: 6 feet 2, 170 pounds

Birth Date: January 31, 1947

Teams: New York Mets (1966, 1968–71)
California Angels (1972–79)
Houston Astros (1980–88)
Texas Rangers (1989–93)

All-Star Games: 1972, 1973, 1975, 1977, 1979,
1981, 1985, 1989

ROGER CLEMENS

A pitcher does not get nicknamed "The Rocket" because he throws tricky breaking balls. He gets that nickname by throwing a fastball that looks like a rocket ship. And that is exactly what Roger "The Rocket" Clemens did for nearly a quarter century.

The burly right-hander won a record seven Cy Young Awards in his 24 seasons in the majors. Through 2013, no other hurler had won more than five. Clemens also won a total of 354 games. And his 4,672 strikeouts were the third most in baseball history through 2013.

Yet the "Rocket" in Clemens did not apply to just his heater or his eye-popping numbers. Standing on the mound, the 6-foot-4 Clemens threw the baseball like he was mad at it. And sometimes he was indeed mad. That showed in the 2000 World Series.

Roger Clemens won seven Cy Young Awards between 1986 and 2004.

Clemens starred for the New York Yankees. But he had angered New York Mets catcher Mike Piazza when he had hit Piazza earlier that season.

The two teams again met in the Fall Classic. This time Piazza swung so hard at Clemens's pitch that his bat broke in half while hitting a foul ball. Clemens grabbed the bat and threw it—right at Piazza's feet!

"There was no intent," Clemens said afterward. "I was fired up and emotional."

Clemens showed amazing longevity. He won his first Cy Young Award in 1986 and his last in 2004. But baseball fans soon became less impressed by that feat. Late in his career, Clemens faced charges that he used illegal performance-enhancing drugs (PEDs). He insisted he never did anything wrong. However, the PED connection stained his legacy in the eyes of many fans.

192

The number of wins Clemens collected while pitching for the Boston Red Sox from 1984 to 1996, tying him with Cy Young for the most wins in team history.

Roger Clemens helped the New York Yankees reach the World Series four times in five seasons between 1999 and 2003.

ROGER CLEMENS

Hometown: Dayton, Ohio

Height, Weight: 6 feet 4, 205 pounds

Birth Date: August 4, 1962

Teams: Boston Red Sox (1984–96)
Toronto Blue Jays (1997–98)
New York Yankees (1999–2003, 2007)
Houston Astros (2004–06)

All-Star Games: 1986, 1988, 1990, 1991, 1992, 1997, 1998, 2001, 2003, 2004, 2005

Cy Young Awards: 1986, 1987, 1991, 1997, 1998, 2001, 2004

MVP Award: 1986

GREG MADDUX

Greg Maddux did not look like a baseball player. He was average height and kind of skinny. And when he threw the ball, it did not whiz by players like a racecar.

Maddux looked more like a teacher. And in a way, he was. The guy they called "The Professor" relied on his baseball smarts and his precise control to make batters look silly.

Maddux won four straight Cy Young Awards between 1992 and 1996 while pitching for the Chicago Cubs and the Atlanta Braves. His best year came in 1995 with the Braves. Maddux's record that season was an unbelievable 19–2, and the Braves won the World Series.

The key to Maddux's success was in trying to force batters to spend most of their time thinking instead of swinging.

Atlanta Braves pitcher Greg Maddux helped his team win the NL East nine times in a row from 1995 to 2003.

"Sometimes he knows what he's going to throw two pitches ahead," Atlanta teammate John Smoltz said about Maddux. "He makes it look like guys are swinging foam bats out there."

Unlike most pitchers, Maddux did not mind if batters got hits off him. He just made sure they were not home runs. Maddux never led the majors in strikeouts. He only topped 200 strikeouts in a season once. Instead, he trusted his defense to make plays behind him. And he worked quickly. Many major league games can last three hours. Yet on nights when Maddux was rolling, the game could be over in two.

"I could probably throw harder if I wanted, but why?" Maddux said. "When they're in a jam, a lot of pitchers try to throw harder. Me, I try to locate better."

And nobody located better than the Professor.

18

The record number of Gold Gloves Maddux won. The Gold Glove is given every year to the best fielder at their position.

Greg Maddux pitches for the Chicago Cubs during a 2006 game against the Houston Astros.

GREG MADDUX

Hometown: San Angelo, Texas

Height, Weight: 6 feet, 170 pounds

Birth Date: April 14, 1966

Teams: Chicago Cubs (1986–92, 2004–06)
Atlanta Braves (1993–2003)
Los Angeles Dodgers (2006, 2008)
San Diego Padres (2007–08)

All-Star Games: 1988, 1992, 1994, 1995, 1996, 1997, 1998, 2000

Cy Young Awards: 1992, 1993, 1994, 1995

Gold Gloves: 1990, 1991, 1992, 1993, 1994, 1995, 1996, 1997, 1998, 1999, 2000, 2001, 2002, 2004, 2005, 2006, 2007, 2008

RANDY
JOHNSON

At 6 feet 10, Randy Johnson looked down—way down—on opposing batters. And when he stepped toward home plate, he took a big step. To the batter, it seemed like Johnson was halfway to home plate before he let go of the pitch. And it certainly did not help that Johnson's fastball would sometimes reach 100 miles per hour (161 km/h). That combination made the man they called "Big Unit" a devastating pitcher.

Johnson pitched two no-hitters in his 22-year career. One of them was a perfect game in 2004 while pitching for the Arizona Diamondbacks. In total, Johnson collected 303 victories between 1988 and 2009. He also won five Cy Young Awards and a World Series.

Arizona Diamondbacks pitcher Randy Johnson fires a pitch against the New York Mets during a 2007 game.

Johnson's defining moment came with the Diamondbacks in the 2001 World Series. The opposing New York Yankees had won the previous three Fall Classics. They were heavy favorites to make it four in a row. But Johnson and the Diamondbacks had other ideas.

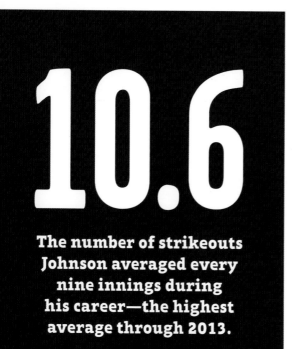

10.6

The number of strikeouts Johnson averaged every nine innings during his career—the highest average through 2013.

Johnson won Games 2 and 6. He then found the strength to enter Game 7 in the eighth inning as a relief pitcher. Arizona was down by one run at the time. But Johnson held the Yankees scoreless for an inning and a third. Meanwhile, the Diamondbacks hitters added two runs. Arizona won 3–2. Since Johnson was on the mound, he ended up as the winning pitcher.

Johnson continued to pitch into his 40s. In 22 seasons, he struck out 4,875 batters. Fittingly, he ended his career in 2009 with a strikeout in his last major league pitch.

"I really wanted to go out on my terms," Johnson said.

Randy Johnson, known as "Big Unit," was one of baseball's most feared pitchers during the 1990s and early 2000s.

RANDY JOHNSON

Hometown: Walnut Creek, California

Height, Weight: 6 feet 10, 225 pounds

Birth Date: September 10, 1963

Teams: Montreal Expos (1988–89)
Seattle Mariners (1989–98)
Houston Astros (1998)
Arizona Diamondbacks (1999–2004, 2007–08)
New York Yankees (2005–06)
San Francisco Giants (2009)

All-Star Games: 1990, 1993, 1994, 1995, 1996, 1999, 2000, 2001, 2002, 2004

Cy Young Awards: 1995, 1999, 2000, 2001, 2002

MARIANO RIVERA

A rock song blared over the speakers at Yankee Stadium every time New York closer Mariano Rivera came into the game. The song was called "Enter Sandman." It was a fitting title for the pitcher who made opposing hitters say "good night."

Rivera began as a starting pitcher before moving to a relief role in 1996. He was lights out as the Yankees' closer from 1997 to 2013. If he was on the hill, the chances were high that the game was already over. Going into his final season in 2013, he had 608 saves. That was already a record. By just about any standard, Rivera retired as the greatest closer of all time.

The Panama native became almost automatic thanks largely to one pitch: the cut fastball, or cutter.

The New York Yankees' Mariano Rivera became baseball's all-time saves leader during his 19 seasons in the Bronx.

The cutter looks just like a fastball.

But the right-handed Rivera's cutter turned to the left just before it reached home plate. To right-handed batters, the ball appeared to be tailing away. When left-handed batters would make contact, the spin on the ball would often break their bats.

Rivera faced Ryan Klesko of the Atlanta Braves during the 1999 World Series. Klesko broke three different bats in a single plate appearance.

"When he throws it, you think it's straight," former player Tony Womack said. "The next thing you know, it's on your thumbs."

Rivera did not get as much attention as some of his teammates, such as Derek Jeter. But he played a vital role in the Yankees' three straight World Series titles from 1998 to 2000. The Yankees added another championship in 2009. Rivera closed out each of those series-clinching games.

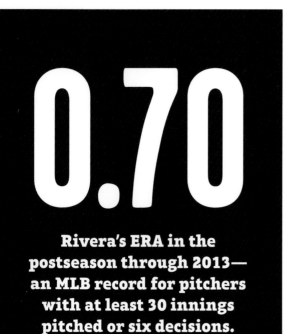

0.70

Rivera's ERA in the postseason through 2013— an MLB record for pitchers with at least 30 innings pitched or six decisions.